# In the Year 1928

By

## Kerry Butters.

# In the Year 1928.

| | |
|---|---|
| **Millennium:** | **2nd millennium** |
| **Centuries:** | 19th century – **20th century** – 21st century |
| **Decades:** | 1890s  1900s  1910s – **1920s** –  1930s  1940s  1950s |
| **Years:** | 1925 1926 1927 – **1928** – 1929 1930 1931 |

**1928 (MCMXXVIII)** was a leap year starting on Sunday (dominical letter AG) of the Gregorian calendar and a leap year starting on Saturday (dominical letter BA) of the Julian calendar, the 1928th year of the Common Era (CE) and *Anno Domini* (AD) designations, the 928th year of the 2nd millennium, the 28th year of the 20th century, and the 9th year of the 1920s decade. Note that the Julian day for 1928 is 13 calendar days difference, which continued to be used from 1582 until the complete conversion of the Gregorian calendar was entirely done in 1929.

A 1928 Ford Model A

# Contents

- 1 Events
- 2 Births
- 3 Deaths
- 4 Nobel Prizes
- 5 In fiction
- 6 In the News

# Events

## January

- January – English bacteriologist Frederick Griffith reports the results of Griffith's experiment, indirectly proving the existence of DNA.
- January 1 – Estonia changes its currency from the mark to the kroon.
- January 6–7 – The River Thames floods in London; 14 drown. On January 7 the moat at the Tower of London (drained in 1843 and planted with grass) is completely refilled by a tidal wave.
- January 12 – Convicted American murderer Ruth Snyder is executed at Sing Sing.
- January 17 – The OGPU arrests Leon Trotsky in Moscow; he assumes a status of passive resistance.
- January 26 – The volcanic island Anak Krakatau appears.
- January 31 – Leon Trotsky is exiled to Alma-Ata.

## February

- February 8 – British inventor John Logie Baird broadcasts a transatlantic television signal from London to Hartsdale, New York.

- February 11–19 – The 1928 Winter Olympics are held in St. Moritz, Switzerland, the first as a separate event. Sonja Henie of Norway wins her first gold medal in women's figure skating.
- February 12 – Heavy hail kills 11 in Britain.
- February 20 – The Japanese general election produces a hung parliament.
- February 25 – Charles Jenkins Laboratories of Washington, D.C., becomes the first holder of a television license from the Federal Radio Commission.

## March

- March 12 – In California, the St. Francis Dam north of Los Angeles fails, killing 600.
- March 15

  - March 15 incident: The Japanese government cracks down on socialists and communists.
  - Chinese warlord Shi Yousan sets fire to the Shaolin Monastery in Henan, destroying some of its ancient structures and artifacts.

- March 21 – Charles Lindbergh is presented with the Medal of Honor for his first Transatlantic flight.
- March 26 – The China Academy of Art is founded in Hangzhou (originally named the National Academy of Art).

## April

- April 10 – "Pineapple Primary": The United States Republican Party primary elections in Chicago are preceded by violence, bombings and assassination attempts (two politicians are killed, Octavius C. Granady and Giuseppe Esposito).
- April 12 – A bomb attack against Italian Fascist leader Benito Mussolini in Milan kills 17 bystanders.

- April 12–14 – The first ever east–west transatlantic flight by aeroplane takes place from Dublin, Ireland, to Greenly Island, Canada, using German Junkers W 33 *Bremen.*
- April 14 – Two earthquakes in Chirpan and Plovdiv in Bulgaria destroy more than 21,000 buildings and kill almost 130 people.
- April 19 – The last section ("wise – wyze") of the original *Oxford English Dictionary* is completed and published.
- April 22 – An earthquake destroys 200,000 buildings in Corinth.
- April 28 – 28 inches of snow fall in southern-central Pennsylvania.

## May

- May 3 – Jinan incident: An armed conflict between the Imperial Japanese Army allied with Northern Chinese warlords against the Kuomintang's southern army, occurs in Jinan, China.
- May 7 – Passage of the Representation of the People Act in the United Kingdom lowers the voting age for women from 30 to 21 giving them equal suffrage with men from July 2.
- May 10 – The first regular schedule of television programming begins in Schenectady, New York by the General Electric's television station W2XB (the station is popularly known as WGY Television, after its sister radio station WGY).
- May 15
  - The Royal Flying Doctor Service of Australia commences operations.
  - The animated short *Plane Crazy* is released by Disney Studios in Los Angeles, featuring the first appearances of Mickey and Minnie Mouse.
- May 23 – A bomb attack against the Italian consulate in Buenos Aires, Argentina, kills 22 and injures 43.
- May 24 – The airship *Italia* crashes at the North Pole; one of the occupants is Italian general Umberto Nobile. A rescue expedition leaves for the Pole on May 30.
- May 30 – Rookie driver Louis Meyer wins his first Indianapolis 500. He would win that race again in 1933 and 1936.

# June

- June 3 – American serial killer Albert Fish kidnaps and kills 10-year-old Grace Budd.
- June 4 – Huanggutun incident: Zhang Zuolin, a warlord, is killed by Japanese agents.
- June 8 – By seizing Beijing and renaming it Běipíng, the National Revolutionary Army puts an end to the 'Fengtian warlords' Beiyang government there.
- June 9 – Australian aviator Charles Kingsford Smith and his crew complete the first flight across the Pacific Ocean from the mainland United States to Australia in Fokker F.VII aircraft *Southern Cross*. Having left Oakland, California on May 31, they reach Brisbane via Honolulu and Fiji.
- June 11 – A medical doctors' strike begins in Vienna.
- June 14 – Students take over the medical wing of Rosario University in Argentina.
- June 17–18 – Aviatrix Amelia Earhart becomes the first woman to make a successful Transatlantic flight, as a passenger in a Fokker F.VIIb/3m piloted by Wilmer Stultz from Newfoundland to Wales.
- June 20 – Puniša Račić kills three opposition representatives in the Yugoslavian Parliament, and injures three others in gun attack.
- June 24 – A Swedish aeroplane rescues part of the Italian North Pole expedition, including Umberto Nobile. The Soviet icebreaker *Krasin* saves the rest July 12.
- June 28 – The International Railway (New York–Ontario) switches to one-man crews for its trolleys in Canada. The keel of the first 1000ft-long Ocean Liner *Oceanic (III)* is laid; construction is delayed and later cancelled the following year.
- June 29 – At the 1928 Democratic National Convention in Houston, Governor of New York Al Smith becomes the first Catholic nominated by a major political party for President of the United States.
-

# July

- July 2 – Charles Jenkins Laboratories' W3XK station begins broadcasting on 6.42 MHz using 48 lines.
- July 3 – British inventor John Logie Baird demonstrates the world's first colour television transmission.
- July 7 – The first machine-sliced and machine-wrapped loaf of bread is sold in Chillicothe, Missouri, using Otto Frederick Rohwedder's technology.
- July 12 – Mexican aviator Emilio Carranza dies in a solo plane crash in the New Jersey Pine Barrens, while returning from a goodwill flight to New York City.
- July 17 – José de León Toral assassinates Álvaro Obregón, president of Mexico.
- July 25 – The United States recalls its troops from China.
- July 27
  - English cricketer Tich Freeman becomes the only bowler ever to take 200 first-class wickets before the end of July.
  - Radclyffe Hall's novel *The Well of Loneliness*, with its theme of lesbian love, is published in London.
- July 28–August 12 – The 1928 Summer Olympics are held in Amsterdam, opening with the lighting of the Olympic flame. Women's athletics and gymnastics debut at these games and discus thrower Halina Konopacka of Poland became the first female Olympic gold medal winner for a track or field event. Coca-Cola enters Europe as sponsor of the games.

## August

- August 2 – Italy and Ethiopia sign the Italo-Ethiopian Treaty.
- August 16 – Serial killer Carl Panzram is arrested in Washington, D.C., for burglary. According to his confession, "In my lifetime I have murdered 21 human beings, I have committed thousands of burglaries, robberies, larcenies, arsons and, last but not least, I

have committed sodomy on more than 1,000 male human beings. For all these things I am not in the least bit sorry."

- August 22 – Al Smith accepts the Democratic presidential nomination, with *WGY/W2XB* simulcasting the event on radio and television.
- August 25 – Ahmet Zogu proclaims himself King Zog of Albania; he is crowned September 1.
- August 26 – In Scotland, May Donoghue finds the remains of a snail in her ginger beer, leading to the landmark negligence case *Donoghue v Stevenson*.
- August 27 – The Kellogg–Briand Pact is signed in Paris, the first treaty to outlaw aggressive war.
- August 29 – C.D. Motagua is founded as an association football club in Honduras.
- August 31 – *The Threepenny Opera* (German: *Die Dreigroschenoper*) by Bertolt Brecht and Kurt Weill opens at the Theater am Schiffbauerdamm, Berlin.

## September

- September 1
  - Ahmet Zogu, President of the Albanian Republic, declares the country to be a constitutional monarchy, the Albanian Kingdom, with himself as King Zog I.
  - Richard E. Byrd leaves New York for the Arctic.
- September 3
  - Philo Farnsworth demonstrates to the Press in San Francisco the world's first working all-electronic television system, employing electronic scanning in both the pickup and display devices.
  - Alexander Fleming, at St Mary's Hospital, London, accidentally rediscovers the antibiotic Penicillin.
- September 11 – *The Queen's Messenger* is the first melodrama broadcast by Ernst F. W. Alexanderson at W2XAD (Schenectady, New York); WMAK (Kenmore) begins broadcasting in Buffalo, New York.

- September 12 – The Okeechobee hurricane hits Guadeloupe, killing 1,200 people.
- September 15 – Tich Freeman sets an all-time record for the number of wickets taken in an English cricket season.
- September 16 – The Okeechobee hurricane kills at least 2,500 people in Florida.
- September 25 – Paul and Joseph Galvin incorporate the Galvin Manufacturing Corporation (later known as Motorola and Freescale).

## October

- October 1 – Joseph Stalin launches the First Five-Year Plan (1928– 1932 – The average nonfarm wage falls by 50% in the Soviet Union).
- October 2
  - Josemaría Escrivá founds Opus Dei.
  - Arvid Lindman returns as Prime Minister of Sweden , with his right-wing rival Ernst Trygger as Foreign Minister of Sweden.
- October 7 – Haile Selassie is crowned king (not yet emperor) of Abyssinia.
- October 8 – Chiang Kai-shek is named as Generalissimo (Chairman of the National Military Council) of the Nationalist Government of the Republic of China.
- October 12 – An iron lung respirator is used for the first time at Children's Hospital, Boston.
- October 19 – William Edward Hickman is executed at San Quentin State Prison for the 1927 murder of 12-year-old Marion Parker.
- October 22 – The Phi Sigma Alpha Fraternity is founded at the University of Puerto Rico, Río Piedras Campus.
- October 26 – The International Red Cross and Red Crescent Movement (ICRM) is formally established, with the adoption of the "Statutes of the International Red Cross"

## November

- November 1 – Turkey passes a law switching the country from the Arabic to the Latin-based modern Turkish alphabet.
- November 4 – Arnold Rothstein, New York City's most notorious gambler, is shot to death over a poker game in a Manhattan hotel.
- November 6
  - United States presidential election, 1928: Republican Herbert Hoover wins by a wide margin over Democratic Governor of New York Al Smith.
  - Swedes start a tradition of eating Gustavus Adolphus pastries to commemorate the 17th-century king on the anniversary of his death in battle.
- November 10
  - The enthronement ceremony of Emperor of Japan Hirohito, is held two years after he actually took the imperial throne on December 26, 1926, following the death of Emperor Taishō.
  - The MGM lion roars for the first time at the beginning of the film *White Shadows in the South Seas*.
- November 12 – The SS *Vestris* develops a severe starboard list, is abandoned and sinks approximately 200 miles off Hampton Roads, Virginia. Estimates of the dead range from 110 to 127.
- November 17 – Boston Garden opens in Boston, Massachusetts.
- November 18 – Mickey Mouse appears in *Steamboat Willie*, the third Mickey Mouse cartoon released, but the first sound film and the first such film to be generally distributed.
- November 22 – The one-movement ballet *Boléro* with music by Maurice Ravel and choreography by Bronislava Nijinska premières at the Paris Opéra to a commission by Ida Rubinstein.

## December

- December 3 – In Rio de Janeiro, a seaplane sent to greet Alberto Santos-Dumont crashes near Cap Arcona, killing all on board.
- December 21 – The United States Congress approves the construction of Boulder Dam, later renamed Hoover Dam.

- Eliot Ness begins to lead the prohibition unit in Chicago.
- The old Canaanite city of Ugarit is rediscovered.
- Margaret Mead's influential cultural anthropology text *Coming of Age in Samoa* is published in the U.S.
- The Episcopal Church in the United States of America ratifies a new revision of the Book of Common Prayer.
- W2XBS, RCA's first television station, is established in New York City.

# Births

## January

Zulfiqar Ali Bhutto

Walter Mondale

Jeanne Moreau

Eduard Shevardnadze

- January 2
  - Howard Caine, American character actor (d. 1993)
  - Robert Goralski, American journalist (d. 1988)
  - Daisaku Ikeda, Japanese religious leader
  - Kate Molale, South African anti-Apartheid activist (d. 1980)
  - Dan Rostenkowski, American politician from Illinois (d. 2010)
- January 5
  - Zulfikar Ali Bhutto, President of Pakistan and Prime Minister of Pakistan (d. 1979)
  - Walter Mondale, U.S. Senator, Vice President and Presidential candidate
- January 6 – George H. Ross, American businessman
- January 7 – William Peter Blatty, American writer
- January 9 – Domenico Modugno, Italian singer, songwriter, actor and politician (d. 1994)
- January 10 – Philip Levine, American poet
- January 11

- o Mitchell Ryan, American actor
- o David L. Wolper, American television producer (d. 2010)
- January 15 – Joanne Linville, American actress
- January 16
  - o William Kennedy, American author
  - o Pilar Lorengar, Spanish soprano (d. 1996)
- January 17
  - o Jean Barraqué, French composer (d. 1973)
  - o Vidal Sassoon, English hairdresser (d. 2012)
- January 21 – Gene Sharp, American political theorist of nonviolent action
- January 22 – Yoshihiko Amino, Japanese historian (d. 2004)
- January 23
  - o Chico Carrasquel, Venezuelan Major League Baseball player (d. 2005)
  - o Jeanne Moreau, French actress
- January 24
  - o Desmond Morris, English anthropologist and writer
  - o Michel Serrault, French actor (d. 2007)
- January 25
  - o Cor van der Hart, Dutch footballer (d. 2006)
  - o Eduard Shevardnadze, Georgian politician, former president (d. 2014)
- January 26 – Roger Vadim, French film director (d. 2000)
- January 27 – Hans Modrow, East German Premier
- January 30
  - o Mitch Leigh, American musical theatre composer and theatrical producer (d. 2014)
  - o Hal Prince, American stage producer and director

**February**

Jean Kennedy Smith

Ariel Sharon

- February 1
  - Tom Lantos, American Congressman (d. 2008)
  - Stuart Whitman, American film & television actor
- February 3 – Frankie Vaughan, British singer (d. 1999)
- February 4 – Kim Yong-nam, North Korean politician
- February 5 – Andrew Greeley, American Roman Catholic priest and fiction novelist (d. 2013)
- February 8 – Gene Lees, Canadian biographer and lyricist (d. 2010)
- February 9
  - Frank Frazetta, American illustrator (d. 2010)
  - Rinus Michels, Dutch association football player and coach (d. 2005)
  - Roger Mudd, American journalist
- February 16 – Porfi Jiménez, Dominican-Venezuelan musician (d. 2010)
- February 18 – John Ostrom, American paleontologist (d. 2005)
- February 20 – Jean Kennedy Smith, American diplomat
- February 22 – Sir Bruce Forsyth, English entertainer
- February 23
  - Ralph Earnhardt, American race car driver (d. 1973)
  - Vasily Lazarev, Russian cosmonaut (d. 1990)
- February 26
  - Fats Domino, African-American musician
  - Anatoly Filipchenko, Russian cosmonaut
  - Ariel Sharon, 11th Prime Minister of Israel (d. 2014)

# March

Fidel Valdez Ramos

Fred Rogers

Gordie Howe

- March 1 – Jacques Rivette, French filmmaker (d. 2016)
- March 3 – Gudrun Pausewang, German writer
- March 4
  - Samuel Adler, American composer
  - Alan Sillitoe, English writer (d. 2010)
- March 8 – Gerald Bull, Canadian engineer (d. 1990)
- March 10
  - Kiyoshi Atsumi, Japanese actor (d. 1996)
  - James Earl Ray, American assassin (d. 1998)

- March 12
  - Edward Albee, American dramatist
  - Aldemaro Romero, Venezuelan musician (d. 2007)
- March 14 – Félix Rodríguez de la Fuente, Spanish naturalist and broadcaster (d. 1980)
- March 16
  - Karlheinz Böhm, Austrian actor (d. 2014)
  - Wakanohana Kanji I, Japanese sumo wrestler (d. 2010)
  - Christa Ludwig, German mezzo-soprano
  - Victor Maddern, English actor (d. 1993)
- March 17– Eunice Gayson, An English Actress
- March 18 – Fidel Valdez Ramos, President of the Philippines
- March 19
  - Hans Küng, Swiss Roman Catholic theologian
  - Patrick McGoohan, American-born British-based actor of Irish descent (d. 2009)
- March 20 – Fred Rogers, American children's television host (d. 2003)
- March 21 – Surya Bahadur Thapa, 24th Prime Minister of Nepal (d. 2015)
- March 24 – Byron Janis, American pianist
- March 25 – Jim Lovell, American astronaut
- March 28
  - Zbigniew Brzezinski, Polish-born U.S. National Security Advisor
  - Alexander Grothendieck, German-born mathematician (d. 2014)
- March 29 – Vincent Gigante, Italian-American mobster (d. 2005)
- March 31
  - Lefty Frizzell, American country music performer (d. 1975)
  - Gordie Howe, Canadian hockey player (d. 2016)

# April

James D. Watson

James Garner

Shirley Temple

- April 1 – George Grizzard, American actor (d. 2007)
- April 2
  - Serge Gainsbourg, French singer (d. 1991)
  - Piet Römer, Dutch actor (d. 2012)
- April 4
  - Maya Angelou, African-American poet and novelist (d. 2014)
  - Estelle Harris, American actress
- April 6

- Joi Lansing, American actress (b. 1972)
- James D. Watson, American geneticist; recipient of the Nobel Prize in Physiology or Medicine
- April 7
  - James Garner, American actor and producer (d. 2014)
  - Alan J. Pakula, American producer and director (d. 1998)
  - James White, Irish writer (d. 1999)
- April 8 – Eric Porter, English actor (d. 1995)
- April 9 – Tom Lehrer, American songwriter and satirist
- April 11 – Ethel Kennedy, wife of Robert F. Kennedy
- April 12
  - Hardy Krüger, German actor
  - Jean-François Paillard, French conductor (d. 2013)
- April 17 – Cynthia Ozick, American writer
- April 18 – Karl Josef Becker, German cardinal (d. 2015)
- April 19
  - Alexis Korner, British musician (d. 1984)
  - Sultan Azlan Shah of Perak, King of Malaysia (d. 2014)
- April 20 – Robert Byrne, American chess player (d. 2013)
- April 23 – Shirley Temple, American actress and diplomat (d. 2014)
- April 25 – Cy Twombly, American artist (d. 2011)
- April 28 – Yves Klein, French artist (d. 1962)

**May**

Hosni Mubarak

- May 1 – Desmond Titterington, British race car driver (d. 2002)

- May 3
    - Dave Dudley, American singer (d. 2003)
    - Jacques-Louis Lions, French mathematician (d. 2001)
- May 4
    - Maynard Ferguson, Canadian jazz trumpeter (d. 2006)
    - Elemér Hankiss, Hungarian sociologist and philosopher (d. 2015)
    - Hosni Mubarak, former President of Egypt
    - Joseph Tydings, former Democratic United States Senator
- May 8
    - Gregory Scarpa, American mobster (d. 1994)
    - Theodore Sorenson, American lawyer and speechwriter (d. 2010)
- May 9
    - Pancho Gonzales, American tennis player (d. 1995)
    - Barbara Ann Scott, Canadian figure skater (d. 2012)
    - Jean Smith, American professional baseball player (d. 2011)
- May 10
    - Mel Lewis, American jazz drummer and band leader (d. 1990)
    - Lothar Schmid, German chess player (d. 2013)
    - Arnold Rüütel, President of Estonia
- May 12 – Burt Bacharach, American composer
- May 13 – Jim Shoulders, American rodeo cowboy (d. 2007)
- May 16 – Billy Martin, American baseball player and manager (d. 1989)
- May 18 – Pernell Roberts, American actor (d. 2010)
- May 19
    - Colin Chapman, Founder of Lotus Cars (d. 1982)
    - Dolph Schayes, American basketball player (d. 2015)
- May 21 – Alice Drummond, American actress
- May 23
    - Jeannie Carson, English actress and comedian
    - Rosemary Clooney, American singer and actress (d. 2002)
- May 24 – Adrian Frutiger, Swiss typeface designer and cutter (d. 2015)

- May 26 – Jack Kevorkian, American right-to-die advocate (d. 2011)

## June

Che Guevara

- June 1
  - Georgi Dobrovolski, Russian cosmonaut (d. 1971)
  - Bob Monkhouse, English comedian and game show host (d. 2003)
- June 3 – Donald Judd, American artist (d. 1994)
- June 10 – Maurice Sendak, American children's author/illustrator (d. 2012)
- June 11 – Queen Fabiola of Belgium, Spanish Queen Consort of King Baudouin of Belgium (d. 2014)
- June 12 – Richard M. Sherman, American songwriter
- June 13
  - John Forbes Nash, Jr., American mathematician, recipient of the Nobel Prize in Economics (d. 2015)
  - Giacomo Biffi, Italian Cardinal (d. 2015)
- June 14 – Ernesto Rafael Guevara de la Serna aka Che Guevara, Argentine-born Cuban revolutionary (d. 1967)
- June 16 – Annie Cordy, Belgian actress and singer
- June 19
  - Nancy Marchand, American actress (d. 2000)
  - Tommy DeVito, American musician and former guitarist of 'The Four Seasons'
- June 20 – Eric Dolphy, American jazz musician (d. 1964)

- June 22 – Ralph Waite, American actor and political activist (d. 2014)
- June 25 – Alexei Alexeyevich Abrikosov, Russian physicist, Nobel Prize laureate
- June 26
  - Jacob Druckman, American composer (d. 1996)
  - Yoshiro Nakamatsu, Japanese inventor
- June 28
  - Hans Blix, Swedish diplomat and politician
  - Harold Evans, British newspaper editor
- June 29 – Jean-Louis Pesch, French writer

## July

Francesco Cossiga

Stanley Kubrick

- July 2 – Iven Carl Kincheloe, Jr., American Korean War fighter ace and test pilot (d. 1958)
- July 4 – Teofisto Guingona, Jr., 13th Vice President of the Philippines
- July 5
  - Lorraine Fisher, American professional baseball player (d. 2007)
  - Warren Oates, American actor (d. 1982)

- July 6 – Néstor de Villa, Filipino actor (d. 2004)
- July 9 – Federico Bahamontes, Spanish road bicycle racer
- July 10 – Moshe Greenberg, American Bible scholar (d. 2010)
- July 11 – Bobo Olson, American boxer (d. 2002)
- July 12 – Elias James Corey, American chemist, Nobel Prize laureate
- July 13
    - Tommaso Buscetta, Italian mafioso (d. 2000)
    - Bob Crane, American actor (d. 1978)
    - Leroy Vinnegar, American musician (d. 1999)
- July 14 – Ezra Fleischer, Romanian dissident, later Israeli writer (d. 2006)
- July 16 – Robert Sheckley, American writer (d. 2005)
- July 17
    - Vince Guaraldi, American jazz pianist (d. 1976)
    - Joe Morello, American jazz drummer (d. 2011)
- July 18 – Simon Vinkenoog, Dutch poet and writer (d. 2009)
- July 22 – Keter Betts, American jazz bassist (d. 2005)
- July 25
    - Dolphy, Filipino actor and comedian (d. 2012)
    - Mario Montenegro, Filipino actor (d. 1988)
- July 26
    - Francesco Cossiga, Italian politician; 8th President of the Republic of Italy (d. 2010)
    - Joe Jackson, manager and father of Michael Jackson
    - Stanley Kubrick, American film director (d. 1999)
    - Bernice Rubens, British novelist (d. 2004)
- July 29
    - Philippe Bär, Dutch Roman Catholic bishop
    - Li Ka-shing, Asia's & Hong Kong's richest person and major philanthropist
- July 30 – Joe Nuxhall, American baseball player (d. 2007)
- July 31 – Gilles Carle, Canadian film director and screenwriter (d. 2009)

# August

Andy Warhol

James Randi

James Coburn

- August 3 – Henning Moritzen, Danish actor (d. 2012)
- August 4 – Flóra Kádár, Hungarian actress (d. 2002)
- August 5 – Bogdan Maglich, American physicist
- August 6 – Andy Warhol, American artist (d. 1987)
- August 7 – James Randi, Canadian-American magician
- August 8
  - Simón Díaz, Venezuelan folk composer and singer (d. 2014)
  - Jane Stoll, American professional baseball player (d. 2000)
- August 9
  - Bob Cousy, American basketball player
  - Gerd Ruge, German journalist, author and filmmaker
- August 10

- o Jimmy Dean, American musician, entrepreneur (d. 2010)
  - o Eddie Fisher, American singer (d. 2010)
- August 12 – Bob Buhl, American baseball player (d. 2001)
- August 15 – Nicolas Roeg, English film director
- August 16
  - o Eydie Gormé, American singer (d. 2013)
  - o Ann Blyth, American actress and singer
- August 17 – Willem Duys, Dutch radio and television presenter, tennis player and music producer (d. 2011)
- August 18 – Marge Schott, American baseball team owner (d. 2004)
- August 19 – Queen Ratna of Nepal
- August 22 – Karlheinz Stockhausen, German composer (d. 2007)
- August 23 – Marian Seldes, American actress (d. 2014)
- August 25 – Herbert Kroemer, German-born physicist, Nobel Prize laureate
- August 26 – Zdeněk Veselovský, Czech zoologist (d. 2006)
- August 31
  - o James Coburn, American actor (d. 2002)
  - o Jaime Cardinal Sin, Filipino Roman Catholic prelate (d. 2005)

## September

- September 3 – Gaston Thorn, Luxembourg Prime Minister (d. 2007)
- September 4 – Dick York, American actor (d. 1992)
- September 5
  - o Damayanti Joshi, Indian classical dancer of Kathak (d. 2004)
  - o Albert Mangelsdorff, German jazz musician (d. 2005)
- September 6
  - o Robert M. Pirsig, American philosopher and author
  - o Yevgeny Svetlanov, Russian conductor and composer (d. 2002)
  - o Sid Watkins, English neurosurgeon (d. 2012)
- September 9 – Sol LeWitt, American artist (d. 2007)
- September 11 – William X. Kienzle, American author (d. 2001)

- September 12 – M. V. Rajasekharan, Indian member of Rajya Sabha
- September 13 – Robert Indiana, American contemporary artist
- September 15 – Cannonball Adderley, American saxophonist (d. 1975)
- September 19 – Adam West, American actor; Batman television series
- September 20
  - Donald Hall, American poet and United States Poet Laureate
  - Ruth Richard, American female professional baseball player
  - Kirsten Rolffes, Danish actress (d. 2000)
- September 22 – James Lawson, African-American civil rights activist and minister
- September 28 – Koko Taylor, African-American singer (d. 2009)
- September 30 – Elie Wiesel, Rumanian-born Holocaust survivor, writer, and lecturer; recipient of the Nobel Peace Prize

## October

- October 1
  - George Peppard, American film and television actor (d. 1994)
  - Zhu Rongji, former Premier of the People's Republic of China
- October 2 – George "Spanky" McFarland, American actor and singer (died June 1993)
- October 3 – Edward L. Moyers, American railroad executive (d. 2006)
- October 7
  - Muriel Bevis, American female professional baseball player (d. 2002)
  - Sohrab Sepehri, Persian poet and painter (d. 1980)
- October 8 – Bill Maynard, British actor
- October 9 – Einojuhani Rautavaara, Finnish composer
- October 10 – Sheila F. Walsh, English novelist (d. 2009)
- October 15 – Paul Giambarba, American graphic designer

- October 20 – Li Peng, former Premier of the People's Republic of China
- October 21 – Whitey Ford, American baseball player
- October 24 – Mohammad Beheshti, Chief Justice of Iran (d. 1981)
- October 25
  - Marion Ross, American actress
  - Jeanne Cooper, American actress (d. 2013)
- October 30 – Daniel Nathans, American microbiologist, recipient of the Nobel Prize in Physiology or Medicine (d. 1999)

## November

Ennio Morricone

- November 3
  - Osamu Tezuka, Japanese manga artist (d. 1989)
  - George Yardley, American basketball player (d. 2004)
  - Nick Holonyak, American electrical engineer and inventor
- November 9
  - Anne Sexton, American poet (d. 1974)
  - Werner Veigel, German journalist and news presenter (d. 1995)
- November 10 – Ennio Morricone, Italian composer
- November 11 – Carlos Fuentes, Mexican writer (d. 2012)
- November 16 – Clu Gulager, American actor and director
- November 17
  - Arman, French artist (d. 2005)
  - Rance Howard, American actor
  - Anna Meyer, American female professional baseball player

- November 18
  - Inge Bandekow, wife of German industrialist Harald Quandt (d. 1978)
  - Otar Gordeli, Georgian composer (d. 1994)
- November 19 – Ina van Faassen, Dutch actress and comedian (d. 2011)
- November 20 – Aleksey Batalov, Russian actor.
- November 22
  - Timothy Beaumont, Baron Beaumont of Whitley (d. 2008)
  - Pat Smythe, British showjumper and author (d. 1996)
- November 28
  - Arthur Melvin Okun, American economist (d. 1980)
  - Piet Steenbergen, Dutch footballer (d. 2010)
- November 29 – Paul Simon, U.S. Senator from Illinois (d. 2003)
- November 30
  - Takako Doi, Japanese politician (d. 2014)
  - Joe B. Hall, American basketball coach
  - Peter Hans Kolvenbach, Dutch Superior General of the Society of Jesus

**December**

Noam Chomsky

- December 2 – Guy Bourdin, French fashion photographer (d. 1991)
- December 7 – Noam Chomsky, American linguist
- December 9 – Dick Van Patten, American actor (d. 2015)
- December 12 – Ernst-Hugo Järegård, Swedish actor (d. 1998)
- December 15 – Friedensreich Hundertwasser, Austrian artist (d. 2000)

- December 16
  - Philip K. Dick, American author (d. 1982)
- December 17 – George Lindsey, American actor (d. 2012)
- December 20 – Donald Adams, British actor and opera singer (d. 1996)
- December 25
  - Irish McCalla, American actress and model (d. 2002)
  - Dick Miller, American actor
- December 26 – Martin Cooper (inventor), American "Father of the mobile phone"
- December 30 – Bo Diddley, African-American musician (d. 2008)
- December 31
  - Siné, French cartoonist (d. 2016)
  - Veijo Meri, Finnish writer (d. 2015)

**Date unknown**

- Sidney Kimmel, Philanthropist and Film Producer Sidney Kimmel Entertainment
- Norman Carlberg, American sculptor
- George Parrish, retired American NASCAR Cup Series driver

# Deaths

## January–March

Hendrik Lorentz

Roald Amundsen

- January 1 – Loie Fuller, American dancer (b. 1862)
- January 3
  - Dorothy Donnelly, American actress and songwriter (b. 1880)
  - Emily Stevens, American actress (b. 1882)
- January 6 – Alvin Kraenzlein, American athlete (b. 1876)
- January 11 – Thomas Hardy, English writer (b. 1840)
- January 12 – Ruth Snyder, American murderer (executed) (b. 1895)
- January 21
  - John de Robeck, British admiral (b. 1862)
  - Nikolai Astrup, Norwegian painter (b. 1880)
- January 28 – Vicente Blasco Ibáñez, Spanish novelist and screenwriter(b. 1867)
- January 29 – Douglas Haig, British soldier (b. 1861)
- January 30 – Johannes Fibiger, Danish scientist, recipient of the Nobel Prize in Physiology or Medicine (b. 1867)
- February 1 – Hughie Jennings, American baseball player and MLB Hall of Famer (b. 1869)
- February 4 – Hendrik Lorentz, Dutch physicist, Nobel Prize laureate (b. 1853)
- February 12 – Manfred von Clary-Aldringen, Austro-Hungarian nobleman and statesman, former Prime Minister of Austria (b. 1852)
- February 15 – Herbert Henry Asquith, Prime Minister of the United Kingdom (b. 1852)
- February 16 – Eddie Foy, American vaudevillian (b. 1856)

- February 26 – Juan Vázquez de Mella, Spanish scholar and politician (b. 1861)
- February 28 – Armando Diaz, Italian Army marshall (b. 1861)
- March 7 – Robert Abbe, American surgeon (b. 1851)
- March 19 – Nora Bayes, American singer and actress (b. 1880)
- March 21 – Edward Walter Maunder, British astronomer (b. 1851)
- March 31 – Medardo Rosso, Italian sculptor (b. 1858)

## April–June

- April 2 – Theodore William Richards, American chemist, Nobel Prize laureate (b. 1868)
- April 5 – Roy Kilner, English cricketer (b. 1890)
- April 19 – Dorus Rijkers, famous Dutch sailor and savior of over 500 men, women and children (b. 1847)
- April 22
  - Warner B. Bayley, United States Navy rear admiral (b. 1845)
  - Frank Currier, American actor (b. 1857)
- April 25 – Floyd Bennett, American aviator (b. 1890)
- April 27 – Alessandro Guidoni, Italian air force general (b. 1880)
- May 8 – Clara Williams, American actress (b. 1888)
- May 18 – Big Bill Haywood, American labor leader (b. 1869)
- May 19
  - Max Scheler, German philosopher (b. 1874)
  - Henry F. Gilbert, American composer (b. 1868)
- May 22 – Francisco López Merino, Argentine poet (b. 1904)
- June 4 – Zhang Zuolin, Chinese warlord (b. 1873)
- June 12 – Salvador Díaz Mirón, Mexican poet (b. 1853
- June 14 – Emmeline Pankhurst, British women's suffrage campaigner (b. 1858)
- June 16 – Mark Keppel, Superintendent of Los Angeles County Schools (b. 1867)
- June 18 – Roald Amundsen, Norwegian polar explorer (b. 1872)
- June 22
  - A. B. Frost, American illustrator (b. 1851)
  - George Siegmann, American actor (b. 1882)
- June 24 – Holbrook Blinn, American actor (b. 1872)

- June 28 – Leo Ditrichstein, Austrian born actor and playwright (b. 1865)

## July–September

Wilhelm Wien

- July 1 – Frankie Yale, American gangster (b. 1893)
- July 17
    - Álvaro Obregón, former President of Mexico (assassinated) (b. 1880)
    - Giovanni Giolitti, five times Prime Minister of Italy (b. 1842)
- July 21
    - Mihail Savov, Bulgarian general (b. 1857)
    - Dame Ellen Terry, British stage actress (b. 1847)
- July 22 – William M. Folger, American admiral (b. 1844)
- August 8 – Stjepan Radić, Croatian politician (assassinated) (b. 1871)
- August 12 – Leoš Janáček, Czech composer (b. 1854)
- August 16 – Carlo del Prete, Italian aviator (b. 1897)
- August 27 – Émile Fayolle, French general (b. 1852)
- August 30
    - Hugh Evan-Thomas, British admiral (b. 1862)
    - Wilhelm Wien, German physicist, Nobel Prize laureate (b. 1864)
- September 9 – Urban Shocker, American baseball player (b. 1890)
- September 13 – Italo Svevo, Italian writer and businessman (b. 1861)

- October 8 – Larry Semon, American film actor (b. 1889)
- October 13 – Dagmar of Denmark, later Maria Fyodorovna, wife of Tsar Alexander III and Empress Consort of Russia (b. 1847)
- October 22 – Andrew Fisher, fifth Prime Minister of Australia (b. 1862)
- October 24 – Arthur Bowen Davies, American artist (b. 1863)
- October 30 – Robert Lansing, U.S. Secretary of State (b. 1864)
- October 31 – John William Wood, Sr., North Carolinian politician, founder of Benson, North Carolina (b. 1855)
- November 4 – Arnold Rothstein, Jewish-American businessman and gangster (b. 1882)
- November 5 – Vlasios Tsirogiannis, Greek general (b. 1872)
- November 10 – Alexander Trepov, former Prime Minister of the Russian Empire (b. 1862)
- November 12 – Oskar Victorovich Stark, Russian admiral and explorer (b. 1846)
- November 13 – Enrico Cecchetti, Italian ballet dancer (b. 1850)
- November 17 – Lala Lajpat Rai "The Lion of Punjab", a leader of the Indian independence movement (b. 1865)
- November 18 – Mauritz Stiller, Finnish screenwriter and director (b. 1883)
- November 21 – Heinrich XXVII, Prince Reuss Younger Line, (b. 1858)
- November 26 – Reinhard Scheer, German admiral (b. 1863)
- November 27 – Frank Hedges Butler, British wine merchant and foundering member of the Aero Club of Great Britain (b. 1855)
- December 1
  - Arthur Gore, British tennis player (b. 1868)
  - José Eustasio Rivera, Colombian writer (b. 1888)
- December 2 – Hallam Tennyson, second Governor-General of Australia (b. 1852)
- December 10 – Charles Rennie Mackintosh, Scottish architect (b. 1868)
- December 11 – Lewis Latimer, American inventor (b. 1848)
- December 14

- Theodore Roberts, American actor (b. 1861)
  - Pierre Ruffey, French general (b. 1851)
- December 16 – Elinor Wylie, American poet and novelist (b. 1885)
- December 17 – Eglantyne Jebb, English human rights activist and co-founder of *Save the Children* (b. 1876)
- December 21 – Luigi Cadorna, Italian general (b. 1850)
- December 25 – Fred Thomson, American silent film actor (b. 1890)

## Nobel Prizes

- Physics – Owen Willans Richardson
- Chemistry – Adolf Otto Reinhold Windaus
- Physiology or Medicine – Charles Jules Henri Nicolle
- Literature – Sigrid Undset
- Peace – not awarded

## In fiction

- This year is the setting of the video game *Blood* (1997) retroactively dated in the game's sequel *Blood II: The Chosen* (1998)
- This is the year that the Stargate is discovered in Giza, Egypt, near the Great Pyramids, as seen in the film *Stargate* (1994).

# In the News

**The cartoon star** Mickey Mouse appears on November 18th in Steamboat Willie.

**Lady Chatterley's Lover** is banned for being to explicit in England and the US.

**Aviator Amelia Earhart** becomes the first woman to successfully fly in an aircraft across the Atlantic Ocean.

**Alexander Fleming** discovered penicillin in and changed the world of modern medicines by introducing the age of antibiotics and his discovery of penicillin has, and still, saves millions of people.

**Charles Lindbergh** receives the Congressional Medal of Honor for his non-stop transatlantic flight in the previous year.

**The U.K.** passes Equal Franchise Act to make the voting age the same for men and women.

**Japan** Breaks off relations with China following the attacks in China by Japanese.

Printed in Great Britain
by Amazon